Discovering
Music Theory

THE ABRSM GRADE 1 ANSWER BOOK

Page layout and music processing by John Rogers – Top Score Music
Music origination for practice exam paper: model answers by Pete Readman
Cover illustration by Andy Potts

Music examples are written by the author unless otherwise stated. Some music examples have been adapted to suit learning requirements.

First published in 2020 by ABRSM (Publishing) Ltd, a wholly owned subsidiary of ABRSM
© 2020 by The Associated Board of the Royal Schools of Music

ISBN 978 1 78601 350 7
AB 4015

Printed in England by Page Bros (Norwich) Ltd, on materials from sustainable sources.
P14804

CONTENTS

USING THE ANSWER BOOK

- Answers are given in the same order and, where possible, in the same layout as in the Workbook, making it easy to match answer to question.

- Where it is necessary to show the answer on a stave, the original stave is printed in grey with the answer shown in black.

- Alternative answers are separated by an oblique stroke (/) or by *or*. Content that may correctly form part of an answer is shown in brackets.

- For more information on how theory papers are marked and some general advice on taking theory exams, please refer to www.abrsm.org/theory.

1 RHYTHM (PART 1)

Exercise 1

Name of note	Looks like	How many counts?
Semibreve	o	4
Minim (*or* half note)	♩	2
Crotchet	♩ (*or* ⌐)	1
Quaver (*or* 8th note)	♪ (*or* ♭)	½

Exercise 2

a

b

c   crotchet   quaver   semibreve

d   2 counts   1 count   4 counts

e   3 counts   2 counts   1 count

Exercise 3

a   ♩ + ♩ = 𝅗𝅥

b   𝅗𝅥 + 𝅗𝅥 = 𝅝

c   ♪ + ♪ = ♩

d   𝅗𝅥 + ♩ + ♩ = 𝅝

e   ♪ + ♪ + ♩ = 𝅗𝅥

f   ♫ + ♩ + 𝅗𝅥 = 𝅝

g   ♫ + ♫ = 𝅗𝅥

h   𝅗𝅥 − ♫ = ♩

i   𝅗𝅥 − ♪ = ♪

Exercise 4

a   Beats: 1 2 1 2 1 2 1 2

b   Beats: 1 2 3 1 2 3 1 2 3

c   Beats: 1 2 3 4 1 2 3 4 1 2 3 4

d   Beats: 1 2 1 2 1 2 1 2

Exercise 5

a   (TRUE)   FALSE

b   TRUE   (FALSE)

c   (TRUE)   FALSE

d   TRUE   (FALSE)

e   (TRUE)   FALSE

Exercise 6

a

b

c

d

Exercise 7

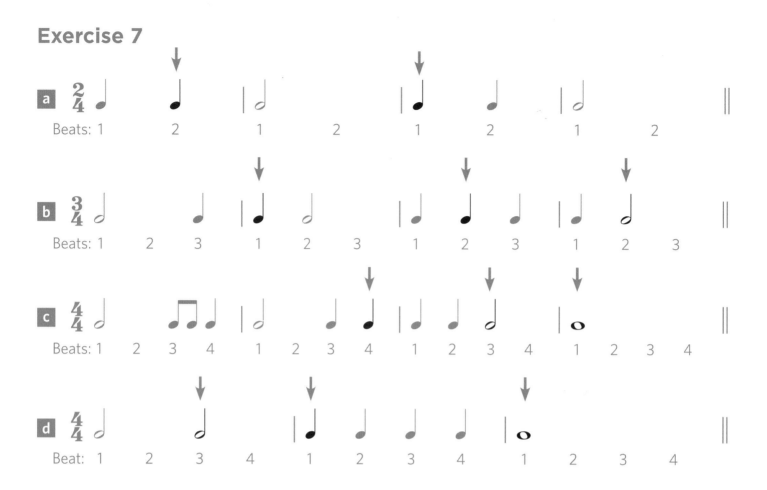

Exercise 8

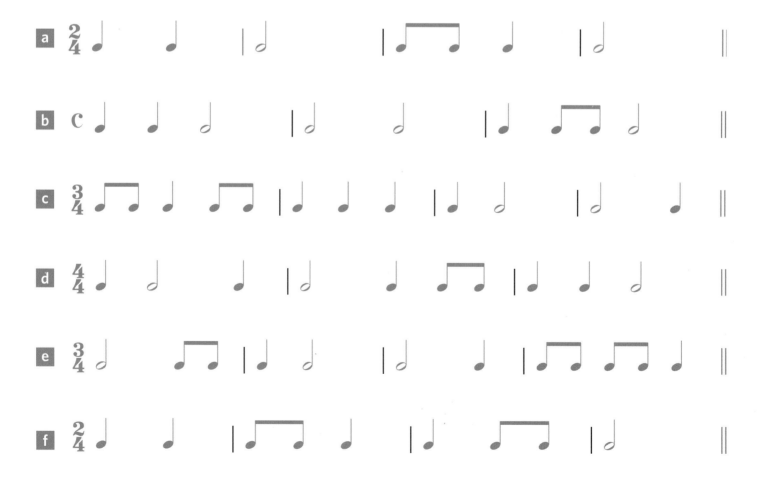

2 PITCH (PART 1)

Exercise 1

Exercise 2

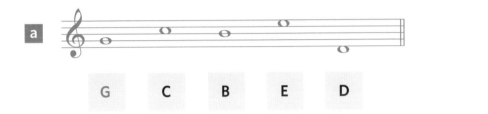

| G | C | B | E | D |

Exercise 3

Exercise 4

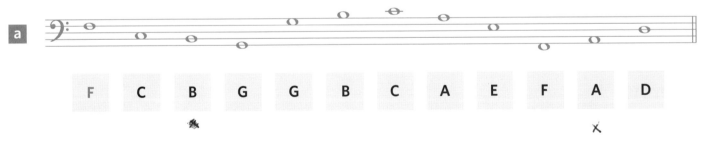

| F | C | B | G | G | B | C | A | E | F | A | D |

Exercise 5

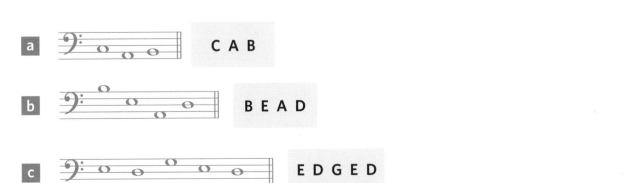

Exercise 6

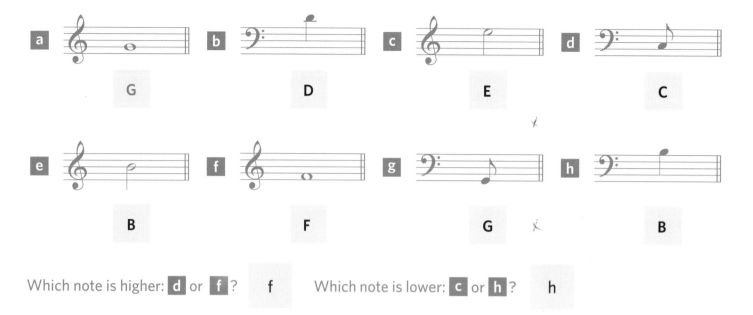

a	b	c	d
G	D	E	C

e	f	g	h
B	F	G	B

Which note is higher: **d** or **f** ?   f   Which note is lower: **c** or **h** ?   h

Exercise 7

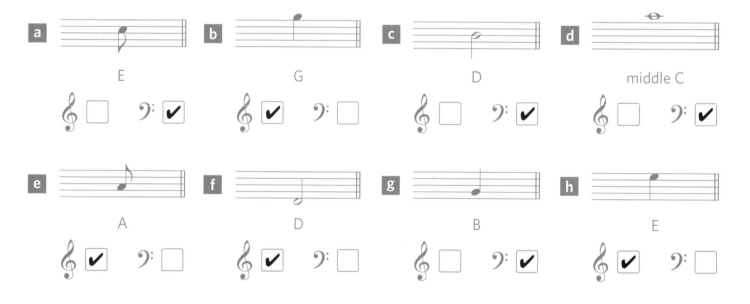

Exercise 8

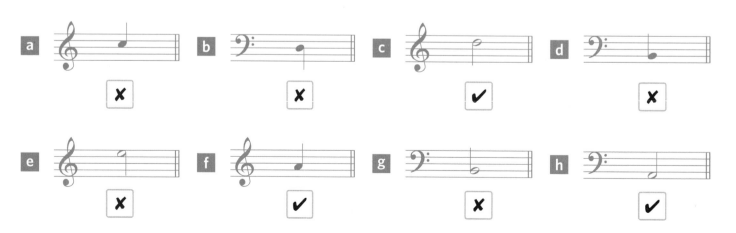

Exercise 9

a   ✘   b   ✔   c   ✘   d   ✔

3 RHYTHM (PART 2)

Exercise 1

a   (TRUE)   FALSE

b   TRUE   (FALSE)

c   TRUE   (FALSE)

d   (TRUE)   FALSE

e   (TRUE)   FALSE

Exercise 2

a   ♪ + ♪ = ♪

b   𝅗𝅥 + ♬♬ + ♬♬ = 𝅝

c   ♪ + ♪ + ♬ = ♩

d   𝅗𝅥 + ♫ + ♬ = 𝅝

e   𝅗𝅥 + ♩ + ♬ = 𝅝

Exercise 3

a

Beats: 1 2 1 2 1 2

b

Beats: 1 2 3 4

c

Beats: 1 2 3 4 1 2 3 4

d

Beats: 1 2 1 2

e

Beats: 1 2 3 1 2 3

Exercise 4

a

Beats: 1 2 3 4

Beats: 1 2 3 4

Beats: 1 2 3 4

b

Beats: 1 2 3

Beats: 1 2 3

Beats: 1 2 3

c

Beats: 1 2

Beats: 1 2

Beats: 1 2

Exercise 4 Continued.

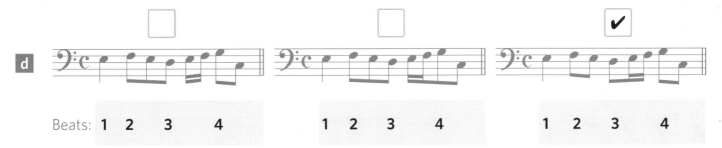

Beats: **1 2 3 4**   **1 2 3 4**   **1 2 3 4**

Exercise 5

Name of note	Note looks like	Rest looks like	How many beats?
Semibreve	𝅝	▬	4
Minim (*or half note*)	𝅗𝅥	▬	2
Crotchet (*or quarter note*)	𝅘𝅥	𝄽	1
Quaver	𝅘𝅥𝅮	𝄾	½
Semiquaver (*or 16th note*)	𝅘𝅥𝅯	𝄿	¼

Exercise 6

✘   ✔   ✔   ✘

Exercise 7

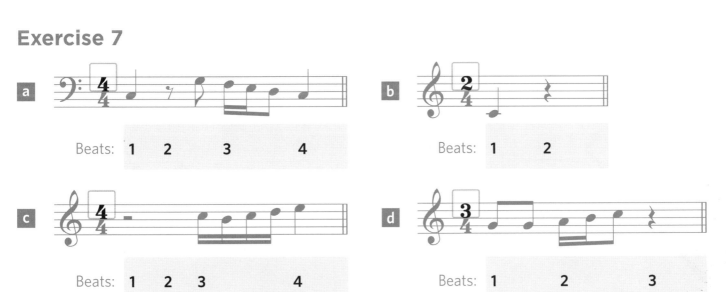

Beats: **1 2 3 4**   Beats: **1 2**

Beats: **1 2 3 4**   Beats: **1 2 3**

Exercise 8

Exercise 9

4 PITCH (PART 2)

Exercise 1

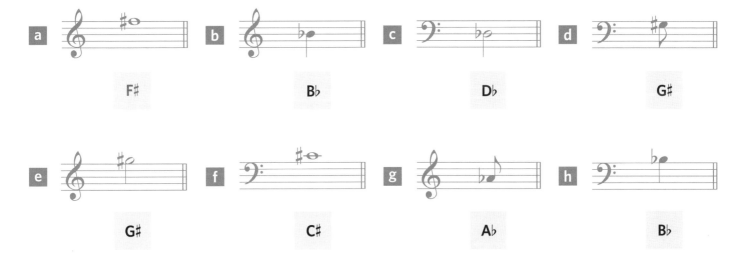

a — F# b — B♭ c — D♭ d — G#

e — G# f — C# g — A♭ h — B♭

Exercise 2

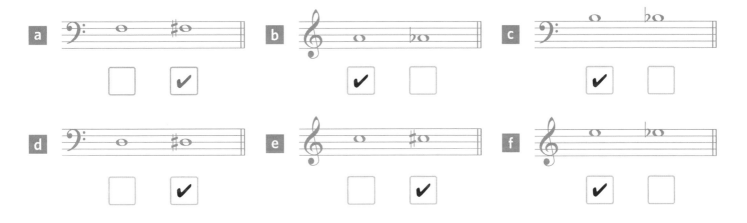

Exercise 3

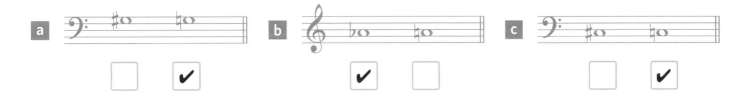

Exercise 4

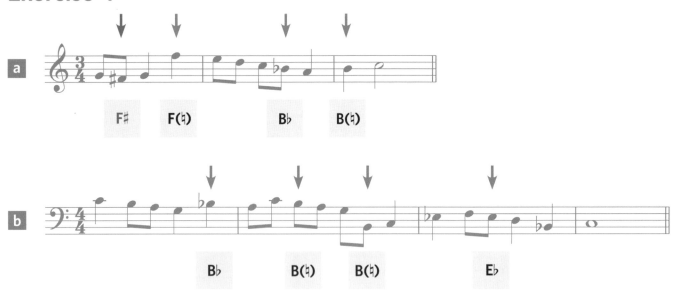

Exercise 5

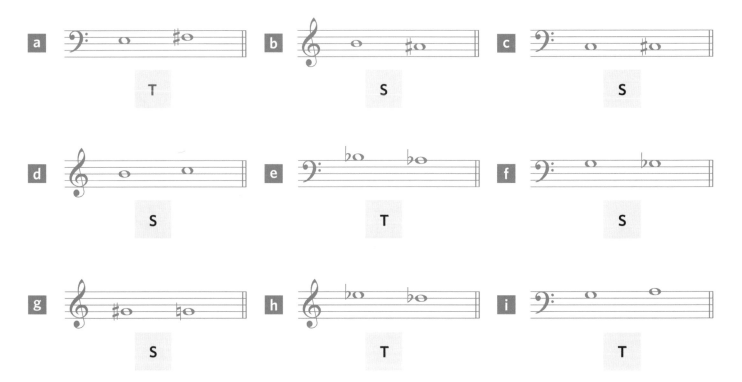

Exercise 6

5 RHYTHM (PART 3)

Exercise 1

a	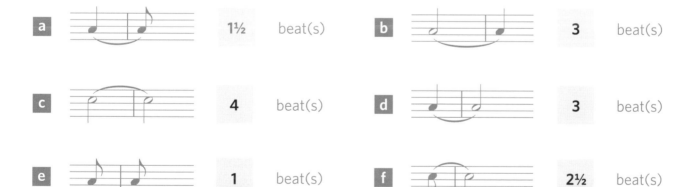	1½	beat(s)

a — 1½ beat(s)
b — 3 beat(s)
c — 4 beat(s)
d — 3 beat(s)
e — 1 beat(s)
f — 2½ beat(s)

Exercise 2

a
b
c
d
e
f

Exercise 3

1 2 3 1 2 3

1 2 1 2 1 2

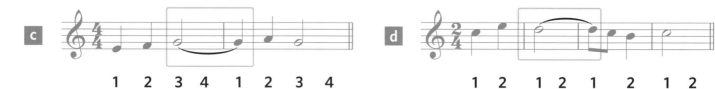

1 2 3 4 1 2 3 4

1 2 1 2 1 2 1 2

1 2 3 1 2 3

1 2 3 4 1 2 3 4

Exercise 4

Exercise 5

Exercise 6

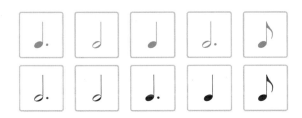

a ♪ + ♩. = [♩]

b ♩ + ♩. + ♪ = [𝅝]

c ♩ + ♫ + ♩. + ♪ = [♩.]

Exercise 7

Exercise 8

Exercise 9

Exercise 10

6 SCALES

Exercise 1

C major, descending

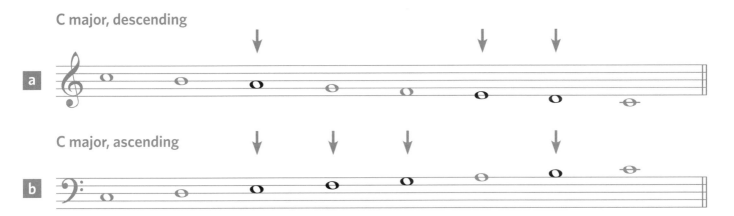

C major, ascending

Exercise 2

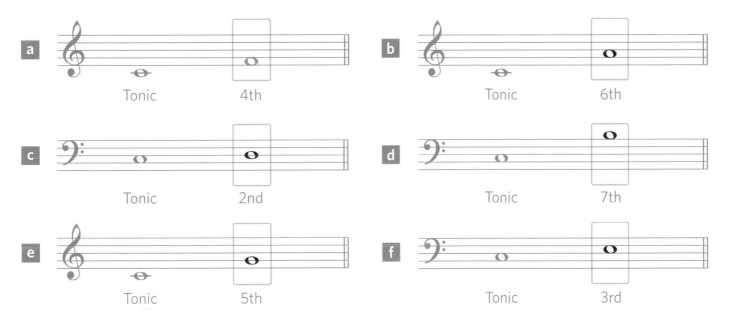

Exercise 3

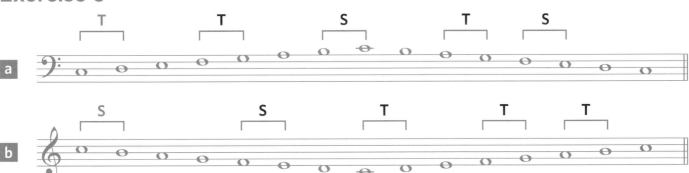

Exercise 4

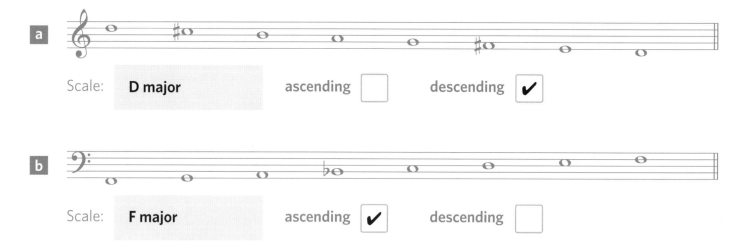

a

Scale: **D major**   ascending ☐   descending ✔

b

Scale: **F major**   ascending ✔   descending ☐

Exercise 5

G major, descending

a

F major, descending

b

D major, ascending

c

Exercise 6

a   (D)   C   A

b   C#   (F#)   F

c   B♭   G   (E)

d   5th   (4th)   3rd

e   2nd   3rd   (7th)

f   6th   (4th)   2nd

Exercise 7

F major, descending

a

G major, ascending

b

D major, ascending

c

7 KEYS & KEY SIGNATURES

Exercise 1

a Key: **F** major

b Key: **C** major

c Key: **D** major

d Key: **G** major

Exercise 2

a G major

b F major

c D major

Exercise 3

Exercise 4

Exercise 5

Exercise 6

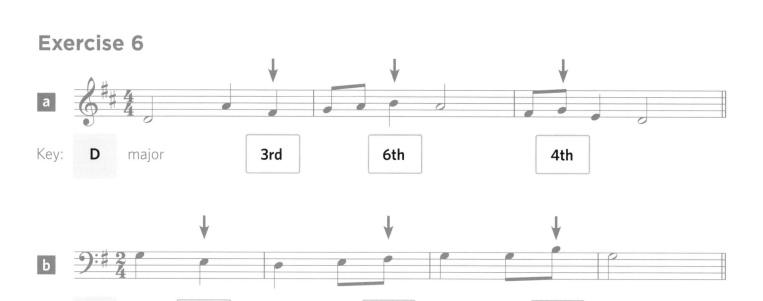

Key: **D** major · 3rd · 6th · 4th

Key: **G** major · 6th · 7th · 3rd

Exercise 7

F# · B(♮) · F(♮) · G

F# · A · C# · C(♮)

C · B♭ · F# · F(♮)

8 INTERVALS

Exercise 1

F major

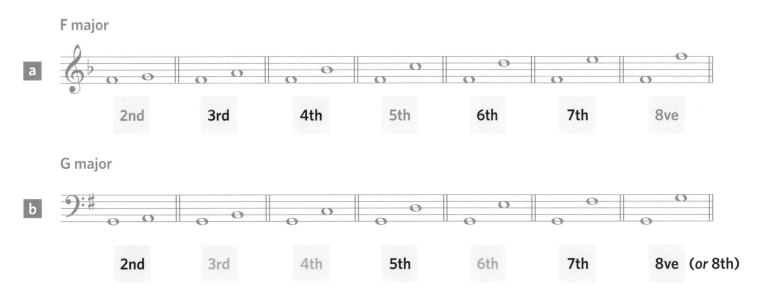

G major

| 2nd | 3rd | 4th | 5th | 6th | 7th | 8ve *(or 8th)* |

Exercise 2

D major

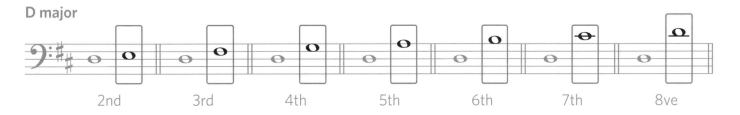

2nd   3rd   4th   5th   6th   7th   8ve

Exercise 3

C major

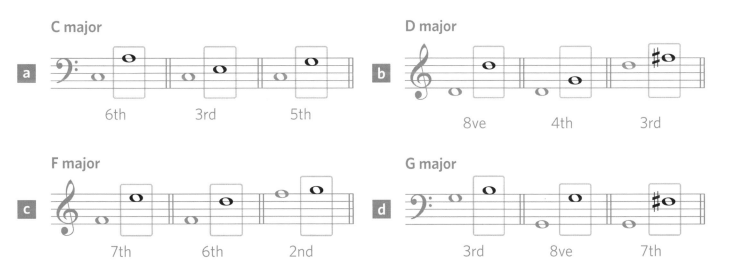

6th   3rd   5th

D major

8ve   4th   3rd

F major

7th   6th   2nd

G major

3rd   8ve   7th

Exercise 4

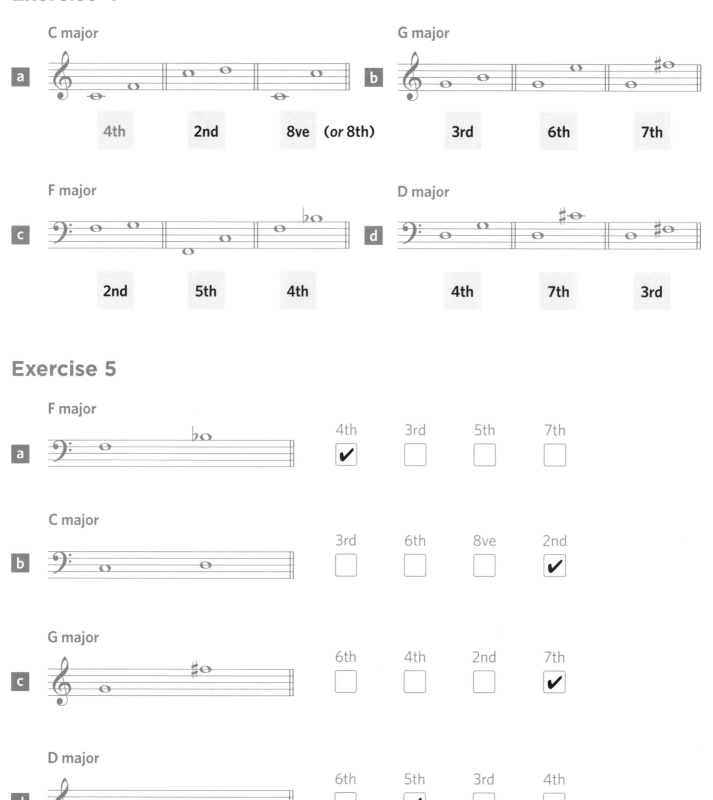

C major

a 4th 2nd 8ve (or 8th)

G major

b 3rd 6th 7th

F major

c 2nd 5th 4th

D major

d 4th 7th 3rd

Exercise 5

F major

a 4th ✔ 3rd 5th 7th

C major

b 3rd 6th 8ve 2nd ✔

G major

c 6th 4th 2nd 7th ✔

D major

d 6th 5th ✔ 3rd 4th

Exercise 6

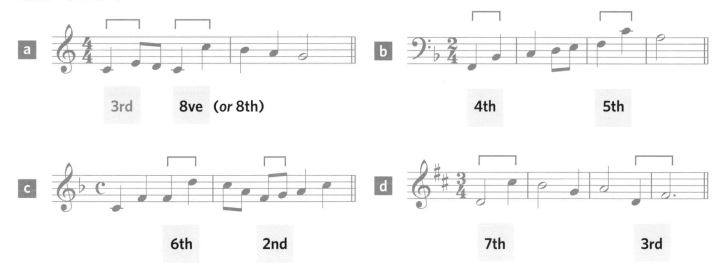

a	**3rd** **8ve** (*or* **8th**)	b **4th** **5th**
c	**6th** **2nd**	d **7th** **3rd**

9 TONIC TRIADS

Exercise 1

a ⟨G major⟩ D major F major

b D major ⟨C major⟩ G major

c C major ⟨F major⟩ G major

d ⟨D major⟩ C major F major

Exercise 2

☐   ☐   ☐   ✔

Exercise 3

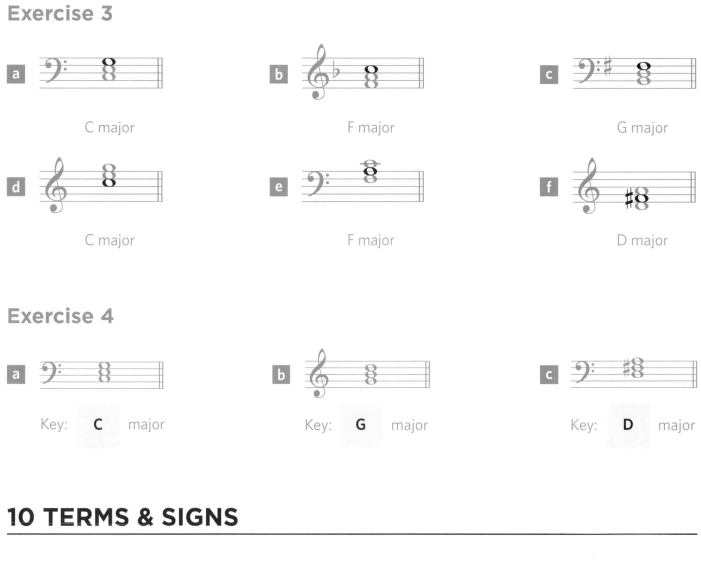

a C major

b F major

c G major

d C major

e F major

f D major

Exercise 4

a Key: **C** major

b Key: **G** major

c Key: **D** major

10 TERMS & SIGNS

Exercise 1

a ☐ *pianissimo*   ☐ *forte*   ✔ *fortissimo*

b ☐ moderately loud   ☐ very quiet   ✔ moderately quiet

c ☐ very quiet   ✔ quiet   ☐ moderately quiet

d ☐ gradually getting louder   ✔ gradually getting quieter   ☐ quiet

e ✔ *mezzo forte*   ☐ *forte*   ☐ *fortissimo*

f ☐ *forte*   ✔ *crescendo*   ☐ *diminuendo*

Exercise 2

a ☐ *adagio*   ☐ *andante*   ☑ *allegro*

b ☐ slow   ☑ at a medium speed   ☐ quick

c ☐ gradually getting quicker   ☑ gradually getting slower   ☐ slow

d ☑ slow   ☐ fairly quick   ☐ quick

e ☐ *allegro*   ☐ *rallentando*   ☑ *accelerando*

f ☐ *allegro*   ☑ *allegretto*   ☐ *moderato*

g ☐ time   ☐ get quicker   ☑ in time

Exercise 3

a ☐ *fine*   ☐ *legato*   ☑ *dolce*

b ☐ smoothly   ☑ in a singing style   ☐ sweetly

c ☑ detached   ☐ accent   ☐ loud

d ☐ stop playing   ☑ repeat from the beginning   ☐ play in time

Exercise 4

andante means:

☐ slow
☑ at a medium speed
☐ quick
☐ gradually getting quicker

mf means:

☐ quiet
☐ moderately quiet
☑ moderately loud
☐ loud

cantabile means:

☑ in a singing style
☐ at a medium speed
☐ smoothly
☐ gradually getting quieter

Exercise 4 Continued.

♩ means:

☐ *legato*; smoothly

☑ *staccato*; detached

☐ accent the note

☐ *legato*; detached

♩ = 96 means:

☐ 96 crotchet notes

☐ 96 crotchet beats

☐ 96 crotchets in the melody

☑ 96 crotchet beats in a minute

adagio means:

☐ quick

☐ at a medium speed

☑ slow

☐ smoothly

dim. means:

☐ gradually getting quicker

☐ gradually getting slower

☑ gradually getting quieter

☐ gradually getting louder

🎵| means:

☑ repeat mark

☐ the end

☐ double bar-line

☐ perform an octave higher

fine means:

☐ in time

☑ repeat from the beginning

☐ smoothly

☐ the end

11 MUSIC IN CONTEXT

Exercise 1

a C major ☐   G major ☐   D major ☑   F major ☐

b bar 1 ☐   bar 3 ☐   bar 5 ☐   bar 7 ☑

c The **longest** note in the melody is a ...

dotted crotchet ☐   minim ☐   dotted minim ☑   semibreve ☐

The **highest** note in the melody is a ...

D ☑   D♯ ☐   F ☐   F♯ ☐

d The melody should be played very loudly.   TRUE (FALSE)

The notes in bar 1 are tied.   TRUE (FALSE)

The melody should be played at a medium speed.   (TRUE) FALSE

The note in bar 4 should be held for three beats.   (TRUE) FALSE

Exercise 2

a bar 2 ☐   bar 4 ☑   bar 6 ☐   bar 8 ☐

b *cantabile* ☐   *dolce* ☐   *legato* ☑   *staccato* ☐

c 2nd ☐   3rd ☐   4th ☐   5th ☑

   2nd ☑   3rd ☐   4th ☐   5th ☐

d Bar: 4

e The **tempo** of the melody is ...

   quick ☑   at a medium speed ☐   fairly quick ☐   slow ☐

f The melody is written in the treble clef.   TRUE   (FALSE)

   The first note of bar 1 should be played with an accent.   (TRUE)   FALSE

   All the quavers should be played *staccato*.   TRUE   (FALSE)

   All the notes in bar 6 should be played loudly.   TRUE   (FALSE)

Exercise 3

a At the beginning, the music should be played quietly and in a singing style.   ☐

   At the beginning, the music should be played moderately quietly and sweetly.   ☐

   At the beginning, the music should be played quietly and sweetly.   ☑

b This piece has a G major key signature.   (TRUE)   FALSE

c This bar contains the key note, or tonic.   bar 1 ☐   bar 2 ☑   bar 6 ☐   bar 8 ☐

   This bar contains two Ds.   bar 2 ☐   bar 3 ☐   bar 4 ☐   bar 7 ☑

   This bar contains a *crescendo*.   bar 4 ☐   bar 5 ☐   bar 6 ☑   bar 8 ☐

   This bar contains a dotted minim.   bar 1 ☑   bar 4 ☐   bar 7 ☐   bar 8 ☐

d Bar 4 has the same rhythm as ...   bar 8 ☐   bar 5 ☐   bar 2 ☐   bar 6 ☑

   Slurs are used in ...   bars 1 & 2 ☐   bar 2 ☐   bars 2 & 7 ☑   bar 1 ☐

Practice
Exam Paper
Model Answers

ABRSM Grade 1

1.1 (a) **3/4** (3)

(b) **2/4**

(c) **4/4**

1.2 (5)

(a)

(b)

(c)

(d)

(e)

1.3 (a) 2 (2)

(b) 6

1.4 Tick (✔) **one** box to show which bar is grouped correctly. (1)

1.5 (3)

1.6 (1)

2 Pitch

14/15

2.1 (a) F♯ ✓ (b) G ✓ (c) B♭ ✗ (7)

(d) A ✓ (e) C♯ ✓ (f) D ✓

(g) E ✓

2.2 (4)

2.3 (a) (b) (c) (d) (4)

3 Keys and Scales

/15

3.1 (1)

3.2 (1)

3.3   (3)

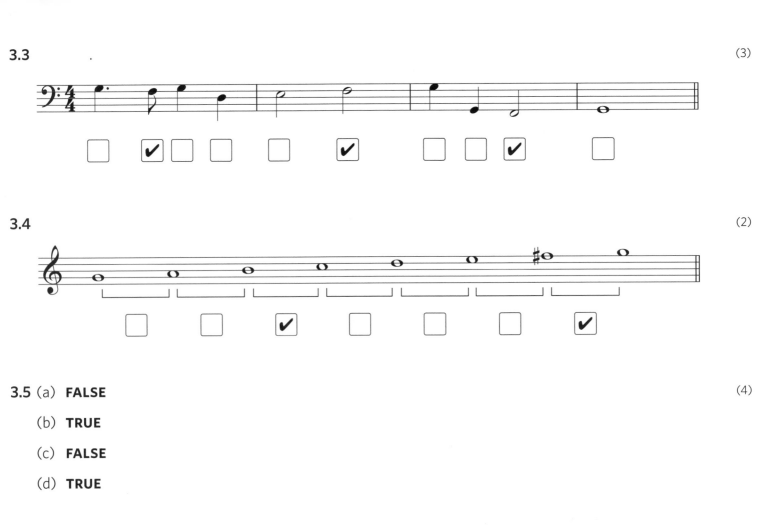

3.4   (2)

3.5 (a) **FALSE**   (4)

   (b) **TRUE**

   (c) **FALSE**

   (d) **TRUE**

3.6   (1)

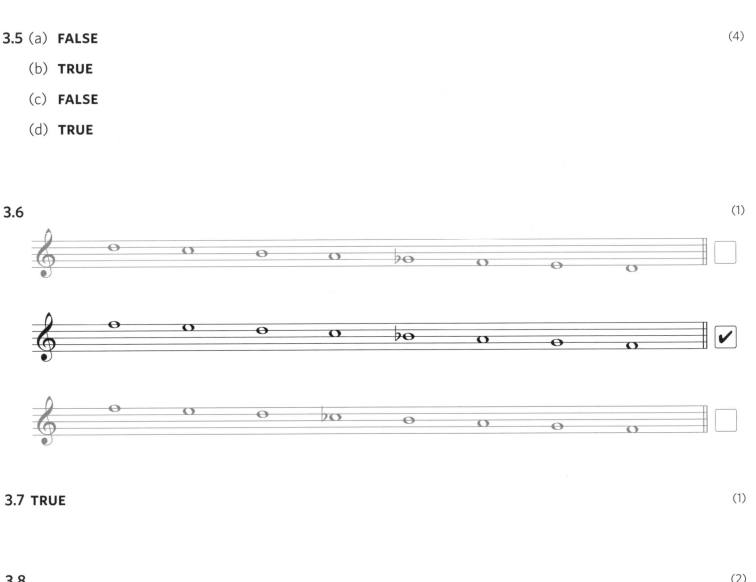

3.7 TRUE   (1)

3.8   (2)

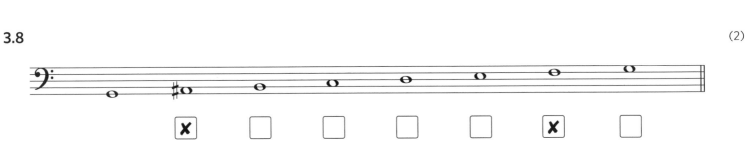

4 Intervals

4.1 (5)

(a)  (b) 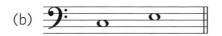 (c)

(d)  (e)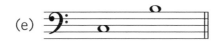

4.2 (a) 8th/8ve   (b) 5th   (c) 2nd   (5)

(d) 3rd   (e) 7th

5 Tonic Triads

5.1 (a) **TRUE** (3)

(b) **FALSE**

(c) **TRUE**

5.2 (3)

(a)  (b)  (c)

F major   C major   G major

5.3 (a) C major (4)

(b) D major

(c) F major

(d) G major

6 Terms and Signs

Andante means:

at a medium speed

Fine means:

the end

⌢ means:

pause on the note or rest

ff means:

very loud

means:

slur: perform smoothly

7 Music in Context

7.1 FALSE (1)

7.2 bar 8 (1)

7.3 (a) minim (3)

   (b) bar 7

   (c) E